THE POETS CORNER

THE POETS CORNER

I've never wanted to suffocate so bad
My own hand pressing over my noisemakers
The edge of my index finger plugging my air holes
With tears of effort dripping down my mask like slime
I was tired of lonely letters written by one's hand in the poets
corner
It depressed me to see them all stuck together in one place
Never to be sent, delivered, or read

I never wanted to suffocate so badly,
Until the day when I was the only one who got my messages
Until the day when window cracks of sunshine are all that
was lucky
There was nothing that I could do,
No space to move away from myself for some time
No way to see other people
No one else around to understand why
I could've fought myself for oxygen until the battle was won
Or continued to write unmoving notes beside myself in the
poets corner
For some reason I choose to live

FOOD TALKS BACK

I learned that being alone is a forte
When you have no one,
Remember that you have food
As long as you chew, it'll never be silent
The more you eat, the bigger the response
Food talks back
No matter what, it always has the answers
Whether you're angry, stressed, or depressed
It can sing you to sleep
Or give you some spicy conversation
With a few cheesy jokes
Food always talks back

Sometimes we talk too much
But it feels so much better to fill the void
Munch Munch, Crunch Crunch
You talk too much
You're full of it
My stomach hurts, and I'm still alone
But my refrigerator is still part of home
You look down at your stomach
Apologizing for you've offended yourself
You're stomach hurts now,
But you're sure you'll be back

Snacktime is always nice
Plus, food talks back

DOUBLE PERSONALITY

I stand tall against the small
I am myself, but becoming someone else
I can be insecure or I will know for sure
Insanely running out of time is what I am sometimes
I've got a double personality
Two people come as one and become me
My brown face is all you'll see
Then open my mind,
And you'll find many colors

As they say, sadly I am a Gemini
I must be fickle, or funny
But I'll never waste your time
I hope we can both earn your trust
But you never know which one you'll meet
I only have half control
Often my splits are very unique
Sometimes I'm the only one who doesn't know
'You're not yourself today'
Little do you know I am
I say I'll do better tomorrow
As I always should and can

We play dress up in each others clothes
We talk about things that nobody knows
Me and I watch the sky
And see totally different things

Me 1 sees the planes, and wonders where they're going
Me 2 see clouds, and thinks about acid rain and snowing
We love to hold hands and pretend we love each other
We're still working on communication
And We fight like brothers
So I suppose I do love me
Both sides, all around, there's still so much to see
Even from my view, I'm still learning about you

Double personalities
That's me and I, I and we
One of us is afraid to swim in the sea
The other fears the underworld, but doesn't mind the water
One of me hates when the other one wanders
Now we both sit here writing, continuing to ponder

REVENGE

I wrote this in pen so it couldn't be erased
So I'll remember it all,
The smells, the tastes
Of blood and revenge, it was so sweet
Until the aftertaste and again..... We meet
Both hands have taken a hold and are shaking me apart
This is beautiful when it comes to revenge,
But it's no work of art
We'll go downtown
We know you'll be around
Sneaking up,
Then pushing you to the ground
The horror on your face,
Your red liquid flowing
Revenge is all that we're knowing

Forgiveness is what we have not
Not for you, or eachother
Just fire burning hot
I expected to be relieved from this
But now I'm simply sick to my stomach
What have I done to deserve revenge?
What if you come back for more?
I remember your soul leaving the floor
I realize my decisions were poor
But I got what I wanted, didn't I?
I look up confused at the sky
I'm now confused if your head is a trophy or burden

It's too late now,
From revenge I'm learning
Nothing more except for how to keep going
This silly revenge is only for my knowing
It's not so sweet anymore, infact bitter
Now all I wish is to be the person that was bigger

GROWING UP

I used to make forts,
And live in magical castles
Where I lived happily ever after
With my dolls and toys,
But surely not forever.
Although it felt not too long ago,
It's a far away time
And soon wrinkles may show
All of them mine

Now everything is changing,
Including my imagination and mind
I live in my own home,
And I take my time
I couldn't wait to grow up
But it's not that great
Handstands and pictures are not things to appreciate
This is a new time
Where toys are iPods, and dolls are boys
TV shows and movies are a little more life like
And I understand new hidden jokes
The ones planted for adults in family movies
Sugar cane candy doesn't make me groovy
No more playtime, work is here
I've been growing up from ear to ear

The filters that once protected me from the world are fading
I have to learn to speak up

Because no one else will debate on my behalf
I am responsible to tell myself to take a bath
I have to learn to keep myself from being taken
I feel as if I'm growing too slow
Like I'm lowkey waiting
For something more that will never come
I'm only getting older, Not forever young

I've simply been in the same garden for too long
I'm a growing bird learning new bird songs
If I'd like, they can include explicit content
I have to guide myself, even if not perfect
Not so sure anymore if it's good that I can do what I wanted
Free will exist, but I'm blessed to have my scruples
My morals, my lessons, and still my loved peoples
Those who raised me and gave me great advice
Good thing I was listening,
Saving lessons for later laid on ice
I can finally open my first can of beer
And lift in front of my parents saying 'cheers'

It's not so bad when you have an idea of what you're doing
Especially once you realize lemonade stands are not just for
children
At any and all times in life, there are ways to prosper
Simply by this time, I just need to know what I'm after
I'm growing up, and I'm surely not done
I still get told to grow up sometimes under today's new sun
What do you expect from a late bloomer?
Positivity and grit are what keep me longer

I'm going to grow up and become much stronger

PAIN PILLS

I needed help as I always had
Scavenger hunting through my own home to find solace
I wanted to silence myself into a never
The bruises and scars I painted on my skin were pain well
welcomed
Only I knew about my plan to end it forever
And now you do too
Don't tell anyone
You'll be too late anyways
Depression has already won

I never needed a helping hand with knowing my faults
But I always got one, or two..... Filling my box
Today, the only words I know are "Ending", " Dying", "Faded"
All words of which are closely related
To the act of numbing and the potion I mix
Now I think for once, will I even be missed?
I shake the idea out of my mind
It does not matter,
I'm still a waste of time
I continue creating my poison,
All of it just mine

I think about the last outfit that I will wear
It's funny that I decided that I should fix my hair
Atleast give them a more pleasing surprise
They already have to come home

To find my closed eyes
I thought anxiety pills, wine, and ibuprofen
Would free me from my own self wounding
Sadly, when I took the mix
There must be some calculation that I missed

Later on that night, I laid with 'crazies'
Some of them were practically just babies
Some had tried to run away from home
One hit her mother
And one went home
I only found 2 like me
All 3 of us sat, examining each others misery
I'm here for my cuts
I'm here for my scars
I'm here suicide
And here we are

It's kind of embarrassing to say that I failed
But not all success should come to avail
I shouldn't tell you this,
But the stomach ache was worth it
The experience I had may lowkey be perfect
Because now I know what happens
And I know I want different than to lay still
Or have pain in common instead of skill

TEENAGER

You're bigger, You're older,
But are you really wise?
I know your heart is crying through your thick disguise
Teenager, I understand
Because I am one of you
You never mean to disappoint,
But you always get the blame
Hanging with friends, texting,
Television, and video games

I am a teenager, I must move on
To bigger and better things
But Mom and Dad,
Do they understand?
We might be older,
But can we still hold their hands?

Maybe not in public,
We got mad pride
But can you hold us from the inside?
I have a lot that I want to tell you,
But judgement is a thing
And some things you only tell your friends
Somethings we tell no one
A lot of things we pretend

Yes, I'm okay

I'm just a little overwhelmed
Just a lot of homework,
But I'm almost to the end
Senioritis is a thing,
But Junior year we know,
Makes you want to run
Make you want to choose the wrong things
Take short cuts and just have fun
Will make you need to scream

College is close,
and you're afraid you currently don't know what that means
What do I want to be?
We slowly require a real answer
This is not 3rd grade,
And a different ball we have to be after

What are you teaching me here?
How to live a life?
I'm still confused on how to correctly spend my time
I'm in detention for saying what I feel
My teacher must be against me,
This is the real deal
But what do we know?
Nothing at all
Since you think my words are so empty,
I'm confused on who to call

I shouldn't be afraid to call upon tomorrow
But these double digits are bringing much sorrow

I'm still learning who and how to trust
In the meanwhile,
I think I'll just finish my lunch

Grumpy

Don't tell me to smile,
If I did it would be fake
I don't like the feeling of this silly, fickle day
Why can't I just throw all the hours away?
The happy and the sad
I'll face the world, I'm brave
But can't I just be emotionless?
Or would that be the easy way?

You pick and you prod,
At everything I do
You're wrong, you're wrong
That's all I hear from you
Have you ever thought about
Turning from the mirror,
And picking on someone else
Besides yourself?

Myself and I have finally come to terms.
We're not allowed to care,
No matter what emotions are there.
We will face the world,
And save ourselves
Me and we will always be our only help
Maybe then I'll smile
As I fold into myself

See, when it's only us
It can only get so bad
Until we get quiet and sleep,
Then wake up sad
She hates getting up,
But I don't mind mornings
We get irritated at each other's confusion,
But it's never boring

Can't we just get along?
Every Side of the bed is extremely wrong
I want you to sleep somewhere else
Because you're just so annoying
You snore
And you move around in your dreams
You interrupt mine with your petty little screams
Stop crying, you weak little pity
I wish you'd shut up, you're way too witty

Get away from me
You go first
Get away from me
Geez, you're the worst
Move away from me
I wish I could
Leave me alone
I really should

FIGHTERS

You never give up.
I never back down.
There's something within us,
That will always be around.
That's the reason we're in love.
This gift given from above,
This unnecessary thirst to argue.

We're Fighters
Star-Writers we are.
And we each are,
Each others lucky star
No one can take that way
But us
Now here you are,
Already dragging it in the dust.

I wish you would give it up.
Yet you promise you won't.
And you never will.
Even when I plead and cry
Because that promise
Was not a lie.

We're honest Fighters.
Wars upon wars go by and by
A peace treaty may be in order

But we're too stubborn to even try
This is what we do best indeed
Here I go, planting another seed
Booby traps are what I like the most
You fall in, and then I go ghost

BULLY

Bully this, Bully that
You try to get them back
Then you become the bully.
You fall into the trap.
After dealing with all that,
It takes a toll.
Your heart becomes it's own black hole,
Just how you imagined theirs.
Isn't that scary?
We all have that power,
I know you hear me

It's ours to use.
We all might have different views,
But tell me when do any of us
Get the cues to bruise others?
It doesn't matter about the colors
We're all sisters and brothers.
Is it starting to make sense?
Yes, you hear me,
But are you listening?
Your head is glistening with sweat,
Yes, you're guilty of it too.
I'm trying to tell you,
They're not the bully now
Then who? You ask.
It's you

SOMETIMES

Sometimes I feel invisible
When I speak and no one listens
Sometimes I feel invisible
When I'm brushed off like the breeze
Sometimes I feel invisible
When the apple of my eye turns for my smile
So tears fall because of my dying hope to be seen

Sometimes I cry
When I don't know if the truth is really a lie
Sometimes I cry
When I get lost in bad and need positivity
Sometimes I cry
When everything goes wrong
But when I cry no one knows because I am still invisible

Sometimes I scream
Just to hear the empty echo
Sometimes I scream
Just to let everything out
Sometimes I scream
When I'm disappointed with myself
Sometimes I scream
When I really need help
When my plans have failed
And they fail plenty
Sometimes I scream until I feel empty

Sometimes I need help
when old friends have bailed
Sometimes I need help
When horror has hailed
Sometimes I feel no good
Sometimes I feel neglected and rejected
From everyone around
I feel neglected
When my voice doesn't sound
I feel rejected
When I cave in and you don't
I feel it all when the rest simply won't

You hurt me
Don't you know?
This here poem hopelessly shows,
How much you have grown on this home grown soul
Good and bad but I stay close
Because I myself am not a perfect ghost
But I'm a master at being transparent
So this here paper is substantial as can be
So if this doesn't work,
Then I really know it's me

Help

That girl you just called fat,
Has an eating disorder
The kid you just bullied
Has a family without a quarter
That boy sitting by himself,
Is alone and needs help
The stranger with strange scars
Has a mom who left
And a father behind bars.
The poor soul who was knocked and fell,
Already feels as if it's locked in a cell.
That cool kid with the fake friends,
They all just bailed
Now their "popularity" just feels like hell.
Don't be afraid,
Be their friends.
Because you will make a difference in the end.
But beware of the pain yourself,
Think if it were you who needed the help.

I'M IN HERE

Can't you hear my scream?
All you see is me,
That seems to warn you away.
I try to yell at you,
And keep you here to stay,
But it comes out as a silent cry.
I'm in here
And I am hurting inside,
But of course, I hurt myself.
Because of my own pride

I run and hide my emotions.
I stay quiet as my heart yells,
I'm in here,
Oh dear Oh dear, See me, I'm here.
If you don't come,
I will forever fear
More detriment to my yelling heart.
I've always blamed it on you,
But really, I'm the one who tore it down
Our work of art.
Please stay,
Don't go away.

I will throw away my pride,
I'll no longer run and hide,
If you can push your anger aside.

Then maybe we don't have to fight.
More than lovers.
Together till the end.
Just come inside,
Because I am in here.

STINGING

It's an opening,
Only for leaving
Nothing ever enters these gashes
Unless it's dirt or salt
And I do not find those to be welcome
I do however love my temporary covers
Sleeves, fuzzy and long
Make me sting
A reminder and distraction all in one thing
Lovely, this helps pass the time
I hear hard words
So I punch my thigh

Physical pain is so much better
Than hearing a lie
Or even hearing the truth
But don't give it a try
It can be a drug
An addiction too
The thirst to feel can take over you
And then suddenly,
It just might not be enough
You've become immune to it
Your skin too tough

So what is it that you'll run to next?
That's the hard thing about running,
You're never sure when to stop

Until you look back,
And you know you really don't want to do that
So you keep running,
What's next?
You're running out of ideas,
Still in emotional debt

Strut

Straighten your back
Show your pearly whites
And do your best model walk
You made it through another minute
Keep breaking records,
No matter who spins it
Until years go by
When you're finally exactly where you're supposed to be
Can't wait to see you strut your stuff
For the whole world to see

And when you make it to where you're going
Don't forget where you can from
Good or bad, you are still the beautiful sum
Claim your throne and your crown
Always be the best you that's around
Stay confident, but never cocky
You are the real deal
Be hard to copy
Be a role model,
And strut your stuff
Watch your step,
For you are your own luck

You get the credit
Your persona and style
Stay beautiful and humble

Pretty only lasts a while
When you walk, let your heels click
Let them know who runs this
But do not step on those below,
One day they'll have their own crown to show

Never be too mighty to listen
There's always more room to learn and grow
And more shine to add to your glisten
There's always room to go more up
Let your stiletto heels lift up and away
From any unrighteous or negative sway
You are still the best you around
So shine and strut like you run this town

MY SHADOW

When they ask about you,
I'll simply tell them that it's a really sad,
Pretty silly, and extremely complicated story
Hoping that they'll leave it alone
Say I no longer know where you call home
Knowing that there's not enough knowledge in the world
For even me to understand
That there is simply glory in this ending

When I cry about you,
I'll blame it on the weather
Or my medicine
Say it's just not working
Promise I'll get better
Say I'm over you
Then later...

I play dangerous games out in the meadow
No one ever finds me here
Within the deep bunch of mallows
You hover wherever I go,
My silly dark shadow

<u>What is love?</u>

Love, true love, is unconditional
Unwavering and strong
It beats, lives, and breathes
Like those who indulge in it

Eyelash to eyelash, Fluttering
Brushing against your lovers cheek
Tickles gentle and precise to call upon
That laugh you love so much

Love is missing them
Trying hard with no victory
Dying in the battle
Leaving a particle of self everywhere you go
Hoping they'll catch the hint
Then pick up the pieces and give them a chance

Looking for things that are gone
Sometimes particles that don't even exist
Calling their name even in dust
Hoping that you'll meet again

Against all odds,
If listening closely
Accompanying every emotion,
Every movement, at any time...
You will find this love

If you hold on tight enough
If you gather those pieces
I'll just love you more

Loving is to feel lonely
It's to experience joy
and pain
Just as love can live, grow, and thrive
...It can die
And it is very capable of decay
It doesn't always get better if you pray
But it does mean that you are alive

See, the special thing about love
Is that you supposedly can't choose whom
Plus, only half of everything is in your control
... If that
Players call it a game,
But later become sore losers

Still love is not all written
It is not fate
It is a choice
To commit to the love you have found
Free will is a thing
And you must not expect them to just
Stick around
It you are angry or sad,
Know that it will pass

Just remember to not lose more
Than half your heart
If love is a game,
You must stay smart

<u>Sidewalk</u>

It only takes a bit of the right poison to take out the right
person
Only a bit of pain to hurt the wrong humans
And some time to figure out you're in the wrong place

I know you
Your swaying walk
Your haunting look
Your crooked smile

'Why dress in all black.
Who died this time?'
I do this everyday
Just to wait
Waiting for my end,
Sometimes hoping,
And other times simply expecting

I think I want to die.
'Aren't you curious?'
About what?
'Tomorrow'
I'm not interested in that anymore
Whatever this world has to offer
I've had enough
I already know enough about later
'Well, why don't you just kill yourself?'

Suicide is sin.
'How about going to church?'
I'm not religious
'Well what are you?'
Alive?
'Why?'
.....You're right
'Right? We haven't even reached a point yet"
I have.

As I walked away
I decided to close my eyes
If you focus hard enough
You feel like you're floating
Suddenly I slip and I feel concrete
Must be the right place

I lay there
... for a second..
I like this feeling.
.....a few minutes pass

HORNS!
A car is coming
Why horns?!
Maybe he can't stop,
I think I want him to st-...
I curl then crumble into the fear
That this is it.

When the car passes
I unfold and join the world again
My eyes are open now
And I see that I'm just on a sidewalk
Should've known..
I rush from the habit of focusing on my mental errors
And think for a moment
Contemplating on my heartbeat
I start to savor my breathe

I am afraid to die
I would like to stay alive

Plenty

Noone has time for petty problems
Well, maybe some do
But leave those hollow complaints at home
The random combustions that no one knows about until
millions are dead
Unnecessary and Irrelevant outbursts
Toxic gases mixed with your breathe and negative phrases

What a grinch, grump, and grouch
Teardrop, cry, then pout
Yeah, the world does kinda suck sometimes
But you should really stop being so wary
Haven't you realized that it's not usually that serious?
Life's not always funny,
But there's plenty of opportunity
To have fun

Sanctuary

Running, leaping into the cool space, then feeling the doors
close around me.
Laws of gravity defy me as I look up into dark scopes.
They appear to be puddles floating above my head looking
right back at me.
Depression never finds me for long
When I am holding the knot at the end of the rope of my
sanctuary.
Whenever I am found falling,
I am suddenly engulfed in a blanket of flesh and bone
That holds me with their most prized tools.
Used leaves come calloused, but sweet and caressing, clasping
with mine.
Gripping, pulling, pushing, wrinkled with time
Carrying things even when I am too proud to ask for help.
The worker bees have come to fix me.
When I am angry, I press buttons to set the atmosphere off
balance.
The alarm is one for hidden fear,
And this is not a drill.
I am the unnatural disaster that comes to cut down nature.
This deep hot temper is ready to burn empires down,
and the fastest way to chill is to pull this lever for immediate
help.
When I am cold, I lay within the prickly forest,
Nuzzling the twigs, branches, and even the thorns.
I embrace every part,

Because I am the wild life that finds home there.
Times that I sneak away to my sanctuary are scarce,
And it's like a new place every time.
Sometimes I start fires within it,
and other times I rain upon its surface.
When I cannot visit my sanctuary,
I miss the smooth blanket of skin with red beautifiers sewn in.
Every tune reminds me of raspy, strained, but trying, vocals
Coming from my sanctuary.

HANDS

Calloused, caressing, or clasped with another.
Gripping, pulling, pushing.
Smacks, pats, and pets.
Wrapped around door handles and steering wheels.
Germ buses they are indeed,
But that is not the reason that we flinch from them.
There is only one reason that they, balled into fists,
Soar towards you like falling stars.
Only when their host is angry or distressed
Do they go on their path of destruction
Their puppet masters brain controls their next move.
Nails long or short, growing to their hosts liking.
Fingers come in different shapes or sizes,
And prints are always unique.
In the center of these common tools,
You find lines drawn into the palms.
It is said that they are readable.
Flip the tools over and check the color you find.
That too is readable.
They come in a large selection of neutrals.
Every now and then,
When dealing with paper,
The tools receive a minor injury.
When dealing with more dangerous things,
Like alligators or knives,
We may lose our tools in their entirety.

Sometimes the factory in which they are made makes a
mistake.
These mistakes leave some without the joy of these tools,
And other times these tools are "flawed".
The first day that these tools are freed from their factory,
They are taken down as a forever growing symbol of time,
Sitting like a garden, only belonging to one.
Germ transportation,
But still we cannot help but to hold on.
Gripping, pulling, pushing, wrapped around door handles
and steering wheels.
High fives, holding hands, and rounds of applause.
Wiping teardrops and smacking foreheads
Communication and tucking in beds
Our hands are our virtue
Keep them close
Never forget, they are what you use the most

ACK IT OUT

You can acknowledge life
Without taking in anything
But knowledge
You do not have to stop in your tracks
Just because someone called your name
And you mustn't bow down to anything you don't believe in
Grow and let every challenge
All pain
And each day
turn into water and sunshine
Let the underestimation serve as fuel
And create a garden of grind
Ack it out,
And never waste your own time

Keep it moving,
Keep it pushing,
And keep what's yours
Leave the rest near open doors
Let life deliver and send as it pleases
As long as you ack it out
You're always in the lead
Trust me,
What she has to say isn't as important
As where you have to go
His shoulder shove is not as important
As what you already know

It is not worth your own sweet time
Keep it moving,
And take notes in your mind

A Human Called 'It'

You treat yourself like a thing
You say that you're no one
I know you're not a robot
And you are truly someone to me

And you say you feel nothing
Then turn and say you love me
I think we're both walking together carelessly

Are you numb, or are you feeling free?

Maybe it's just your silly habit of sacrifice
I think I'm all messed up
And you always seem to pay the price

Why are you so good to me?

Why risk it?
Why must I be worth it?
I don't think I can handle the responsibility

See, if you are just an it,
Why are you so animated?
You are a whole other brain and heart
And believe it or not, scarecrow
You are very smart

You are very much worth

And yet you don't know
A thing has a price
But you are priceless and it shows

If I buy you a new mirror,
You just might break it
You silly person,
You're simply supposed to take it
Mirrors are things, but the reflection is you
Stop fearing the knowledge of your beauty
You exist and we are all so lucky
To have a living creature such as yourself
Let me help you hold the mirror
Please just let me help

Two

My friend tells me I'm too worthy
To feel worthless
Reminds me that I'm beautiful
And that she believes I'm settling for second best
Says I should never be in that place
I know she's right
But I also know what I want
I know this is real because
I wouldn't still be here
Sitting as second in command
I'm SZA on the weekend,
If that

Deadbeat boyfriends are so overrated
I've let you get the best of me
I both love and hate it
See,
Someone's watching out for me
I can feel it,
But I really wish that I couldn't see
I have told my friend my little secret
And of course I know that she'll keep it
But I have no choice
I must remember
Her words about my blind escapade
Happening since December

I do not know why I must always fight
Good advice that I know is right
Once again,
I am alone
Why hold your place when you're never home?
I think and think,
I sit and ponder
Plenty of time for my mind to wander
What if I could have so much more?
Suddenly I am out the door
I will find myself or someone new
Out here in this world
Made for more than two

Do Tell

I can't see into your mind
If you don't make me a movie
I can't feel how you feel
If you don't write me some songs
And if you don't tell me you love me
Then I'll never understand what's wrong

I'll never know
If you never tell
And who knows
Until we've tried

Pick me a flower
Give me even just an hour
Show not tell
That's what I need
To know this isn't hell

A halo over your shoulders
Shines bright and invites me over
High beams, fast stream
It's hard to know which direction
To go
Hard to know if I should come over
And it's questionable if you're on the right track
I'm not sure

If I should just turn back

If you want me to believe you
And to know your story
Please sing to me
For I've pained all for your glory

Hard To Find

I don't find things that are in my pocket the first time
First it feels flat and empty
Then I repeat, pulling my hand out then diving in
I find whatever I was missing
I'm one to wander onto the wrong shuttle
Even worse,
I'm the type to forget my own rebuttal
What's an argument with no point?
I'm sure I had one,
But I just smoked a joint
Brain cells, brain cells
I love to lose them all
I barely think anyways
I simply crawl where I fall
Like a newborn child,
I technically know nothing
But like the adult I am
I should know something

Why am I still so irresponsible?
I used to be smart
Now I'm not so sure
I used to be a gem
Now, no longer pure
See, I consistently lose everything
And make it so hard to find
I always lose everything

Including all that's mine

Speak for yourself

Say what you mean
Before you get confused
Before you get set up
Before you forget

Sometimes the right words only exist for a moment
and then we lose them all over again
And to be misunderstood is the worst
So speak and say what you mean
Quick, before the truth changes on you
Quick, before they catch a lie or two

No one trusts me
And only now do I get why
I can't say I know what I'm doing
So who am I to justify?
To critique or callout
To speak at all or to even cry
I've been selfish forever,
And there seems to be much more

I start to believe myself
So how is anyone supposed to be safe?
I say that I know my place
Then constant pass the thick red tape
On your own position and place
I know I never will
But my advice is cake

Eat it up and debunk my myths
It's an easy kill
So definitely you won't miss

There's 3 sides to every story
And mine went all the way left
All wrong, no defense to build
No wall of excuses to protect
I am raw and I am wrong
I think I'm bad
But I'm just not grown

I've started over
A beginner reborn
I must accept that I only know
That I know nothing
I must restart and refresh
I have a new name
It is no longer victim
It is no longer heartbroken
Not jealous, Just 'Listen'
It is no longer sorrowful,
My new name is up to fate
I truly hope fate is real
Orelse I'm in for another shake

I am a beginner
I am not a newborn
Nor reborn

I'm irresponsible
With the hearts that I hold
and advice I was told
I am irresponsible

Too reactive and combustible
Too "maybe"
Too "I don't know"
Too loud and no listen

Maybe even no soul
Definitely no control
I am a beginner who thinks they know everything
I am a beginner who knows nothing

Crumpled notes spill from the trash
Extensions I thought would last
Never long enough for still feet
And Slow hands, no time for repetition

So if you don't get it now,
You never will
I will eat this knowledge here and now
I will not let it get cold
And even when I am no longer a beginner,
I will still be humble but never fold

<u>Let it go..</u>

You always had to wait on me
Now it's my turn to wait on you
Or to give up
To give up on keeping you

When I wait on you
It always takes forever in a day
And When I send a message
You still have nothing to say
I'm not sure if you're even reading this
But my heart cries 'bless' all around your name
I believe you need Jesus
I know I surely do
Please dear lord above,
I'm not sure if I know what love is
Or if mine is due

I don't deserve the honor
Times like this bring me horror
Single life ain't so boring
Unless you're a spoiled lover

And don't call me selfish now
I've paid my dues
Now it's simply time to get over you

I know you see something somewhere else
You deserve to be happy

But so do I
I just got to learn to release
And fly on by

All these new toys
And I just want my teddy bear
But you are not here
So where?
Since you are clearly gone,
I am not sure where to go
The note we left off was so original
Not really sure what to do next
I've been sitting around waiting for a text

There isn't always a right or wrong
Sometimes there's an agreement to disagree
A truce of understanding
An acceptance of what is
Even if done silently,
I get the picture

Life isn't fair
And I guess that's fair
Because life doesn't care for anyone
So never expect it to understand

The world is ending as we know it anyways
Children can die just like the old
You can burn just as fast as you freeze
And you can catch fire, even in the cold

So afraid of doing the wrong thing
Ends up doing nothing at all
Listens to the phone ring
And still misses the call

TWENTY

I've been 21 since I was 15
Drinking and smoking
No cherry, just another female
No longer daisy fresh
Just a little girl
With grown up breasts
A cute butt for men to hold
And when I get cracked,
I get real cold
Plenty of pictures to make them happy
I showed my precious
That no one deserved
I gave away my present
But there were still lessons learned

You are special
And only you can spend your worth
You are a body amongst others
All on this planet Earth
We sometimes only get one of somethings
And sometimes we don't appreciate it enough
Until it's gone, swept away like nothing

I didn't plan on needing it later
I didn't plan on getting better
I didn't plan on sending my scarlet letter away
I should have never let you read it

But it could have been worse if you stole it
So I cannot be mad or have anything more to say
Except that young girls are exactly that
And they shouldn't be your prey
But sadly us young girls just want to get and give love away

But even back in the day
I still would've known better
At a younger age
I suppose I might've been smarter
When it came to taking risks
I was so scared
So safe instead of sorry

I've held up the light of positivity
The bulb has shined so long
And my arms are getting tired
I'm so tired of being strong
At a younger age
I suppose I'd last longer

At this point in time
I do not wish to care
I am here to mourn
Because there's no one there
Why hold up a light when no one cares to see
Why waste time
Scattering parts of me

Isn't it sad that I'm only 20?

ALL ABOUT ME/ CONTRADICTIONS

Lemme ask you a question...
Have you ever been afraid that someone was gonna let you down?
So afraid that you don't even let yourself think that it's possible they won't?...
I asked you a question,
Just don't tell me your answer.

I didn't wanna come right out and say it.
So I became ferociously eccentric and crazy, speaking in metaphors.
I told him to "Pretend I'm dead".
Saw off the head of this monster we made instead.
Oh by the way, the monsters' name is me.
The spirit world laughed
As she fell down from her the rotten family tree,
Trying to trim another's leaves...

Is it okay to leave her, when she's in need?...
No wait..
Don't answer that.
There's no need to repeat

Her metaphor would be...
A sunflower that grew in the shade soon became a wallflower
That was actually a damsel that was locked in a self built tower.

Let's rest this subject for the hour, and switch to how she
gained power.
Like spoiled milk she became sour.
So behind her concealer she will forever cower.

But seriously,
Is it okay to give up on her?....
When she just wanted to see how long he could last her worst
face?..

... Don't answer that.
I'm not sure I'll like the taste.

Like smoking rooms she's never clear....
You can't see through her but don't worry..
No one ever does,
Not sure if anyone would want to
Even if they could

"The level of doubt you go through is funny"

It's funny because...?
Because my shell was too hard?
Was I too shy?
She's outgoing.
And I'm a........ Why?

"Don't do that, k?"

Do what?

Ask questions about her,
I wanna know how bad I messed up.
I ask questions
Because I wanna take notes
For my next chance
So that maybe next time
I can last a little longer...
In the next life

"Who's that about?"

Oh, the poem? The song? The spoken word?
Of course it isn't about you

It's all about me!

How do you know when you're being rude to yourself?
Or if you're just being real?
Where do you draw the line?
I have no line.
I definitely interrupt everyone including myself
All the damn time

What really belongs to me these days?
Nothing
Is anything really mine anymore?
Nothing ever was.
How do you know what's really yours to keep as truly only
yours?

What's trust when any hand can so easily be dug into your
treasure of gold?
You'll never know.
Do I even own myself?
No.

It's became embarrassing to even remember that I once
thought so
Indeed.
So who do I belong to?
Me.

See, now this is crazy
This overthinking makes me just plain confused
It's alright dear,
They were supposed to

Waiting

I'll always rush to the phone as if love was waiting for me
Only to discover that I'm waiting on love.
Not sure exactly what love will bring,
But still I wait.
Willing it to be pain or pleasure.
I'll take it all the same,
with open everything, waiting for more.
Even after the clock takes his rest,
I'll still tick like a bomb.
Like a gun, like a grenade.
Waiting for love to come and throw me.
Only to explode myself along with everything else that I destroy.
Sometimes I don't even realize that I've been sitting in the same spot
Where love was supposed to land for me.
Sadly, love never deployed
It feels natural now,
Sitting here for eternities for something that only passes by.
It's second nature.
Love laughs as I cry
Tears I'm no longer certain the reason for.